GAP YEAR
VOLUNTEER

A Guide to Making it a Year to Remember

summersdale

GAP YEAR VOLUNTEER

Summersdale Publishers Ltd
46 West Street
Chichester
West Sussex
PO19 1RP
UK

www.summersdale.com

Printed and bound in Great Britain

ISBN 1 84024 487 9

Contents

Introduction..5

Why volunteer?...8

How to decide what's right for you........18

Looking for a project.................................38

Applying...61

The practicalities.....................................84

Further preparations...............................106

Checklist..115

Resources..119

Introduction

Whatever age you are, whatever level of experience you have, whatever stage you're at in your education or career, you have something to offer and something to learn about yourself and the world around you. If you're taking time out and want to contribute, you could find yourself building houses in Cambodia, saving turtles in Costa Rica or teaching English to a class of eager kids in South Africa. The chances are, you'll never see the world – or yourself – the same way again.

But an important aspect of organising your gap year volunteer placement is preparation. No matter what you want to do, you need to plan ahead in order to make the most of all your opportunities. Give yourself plenty of

time to look into volunteering possibilities, and you will have more options and choices as well as adequate time to raise the necessary funds and organise the million and one details that are involved in making this temporary change in your life. The earlier you start, the more relaxed you will be and the more you will enjoy the whole process.

Whether you're a 'gapper' or a 'career breaker' you will have questions about what you can do to help others and really make a difference. It is an important decision and you need to fully understand every aspect of what's ahead of you. We've endeavoured to raise many of the most important questions here in order to set you on the right track. Remember, the key to making the most of your gap year is to be honest with yourself about what you want to achieve and what you expect. Don't do something because all your friends are doing it or because you think it'll look impressive on your CV. Find something that you can put your heart into and you'll receive a lot more in return.

Chapter 1

Why volunteer?

While going straight from school to college and university or working from nine to five every day may suit a lot of people, there are others who feel the need to do something different with their lives. Volunteering is an alternative to the more hedonistic adventures, but that doesn't mean that it won't be fun or that you won't enjoy it.

There are many reasons to volunteer:

- to make a difference to the world
- to meet others and make new friends
- to learn new skills
- to gain confidence in yourself and your abilities
- to travel to other countries and learn about different cultures, and in turn, learn more about your own culture
- to learn about the behind-the-scenes activities of charitable and business organisations
- to open up new opportunities for yourself with universities or future employers by adding skills and life experience to your CV.

How do you decide if volunteering is right for you?

For many people, volunteering is something they'd like to do but often the magnitude of the preparations involved means that they lose interest or give up the search in frustration. But more people than ever are taking time out to volunteer, whether to see the world, increase their skill base, to make a real difference to the lives of underprivileged people or to help save the planet. It's up to you to decide exactly what it is you'd like to do during your placement.

What makes the best kind of volunteer?

The best kind of volunteer, the kind that companies and projects are looking for, is the person who genuinely wants to help and is willing to invest their time and energy into the cause.

What are they looking for?

Companies and projects rely on volunteers to supplement their salaried staff and try to recruit people who will bring something new and different to the work they are doing. You may have the experience required to assist the English teachers in a school in Laos or you may have worked in the building trade during your summer holidays and can read plans accurately and thus help build houses in Cambodia. Whatever your experience or age, you have something to offer if you are willing to work hard and contribute to the project. Overall, they're looking for someone who has passion for their project.

These are some of the qualities companies look for in their ideal volunteer:

- empathy
- enthusiasm
- dedication
- creativity
- team player
- friendly
- energetic
- logical thinker
- open-minded
- flexible
- reasonable level of fitness

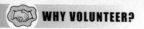

Why do I need to be fit?

You may be volunteering in a remote area and will have to hike to your workplace; you won't be earning money so you'll have to travel any way you can. If you're working with children, don't forget that children have an abundance of energy and don't always understand that you need ten minutes to recharge your batteries. In any placement, you'll be giving your all and will need lots of energy.

What are my prospects after the placement?

Many returned volunteers find their experience was so rewarding that they decide to move back to the country to help on a more permanent basis. Your financial and personal situation will have a bearing on your decisions but you can apply for salaried positions within charities and companies.

You may be returning to a job or attempting to find a new one. The activities you have been involved with enhance your employability. Sometimes it can be difficult to imagine how working with a lion-breeding project can have transferable skills that you can apply to the workplace. The best way to identify what skills and qualities you have developed is to begin by listing the main tasks that you performed.

If you were monitoring lion cubs in their natural habitat in South Africa, what were you required to do to carry out this task effectively?

- observe
- compile and communicate data
- interpret behaviour
- analyse and understand
- take responsibility and fulfil a commitment

It should become easier to identify what transferable skills you will have developed.

Reflecting on your volunteering will demonstrate to future employers that you understand your own abilities and are able to relate them to other tasks.

You can use the same exercise to define your new skills if you are returning to education. You may need to gain particular experience before or during the course of your studies:

- If you're studying a modern language such as Spanish, you will need to spend time in a Spanish-speaking country to gain proficiency in the language. By combining your language training with a volunteer placement, you will prove to your tutors that you can apply the language to everyday life and that you are willing to immerse yourself in another culture
- History and political studies students will benefit from this cultural immersion because it will help them to analyse another culture first-hand
- If you're studying a scientific subject such as zoology or veterinary medicine, working with penguins in Africa or llamas in Madagascar will broaden your knowledge and experience and allow you to take more from your course when you return

17

Chapter 2

How to decide what's right for you

If you type 'volunteer' into an Internet search engine, you will get more than 250,000,000 results. It would be impossible to search every result and unrealistic to hope that your dream placement comes up on your second search. How do you narrow it down? Well, first you need to think about what kind of volunteering is right for you.

Here are a few questions you should ask yourself in order to fine-tune your decision-making process:

What are my interests and hobbies?

Volunteering doesn't always mean making a sacrifice. You can use a hobby, something you enjoy, to help others.

For example, music is a great tool for communicating with others and helping them to express themselves. If you play an instrument you could pass on the benefits of your musical education. In this way, you could teach them something about your culture and learn about theirs.

What about the sports you enjoy? Team sports help people to work together, solitary sports teach independence and self-sufficiency. Sometimes just playing games with children can make a difference; all children love to play and have fun.

What are my strengths?

This is a tough question as many people underestimate their own strengths and often don't consider their innate abilities to be strong points.

- You might be a good listener – think about working as a home help. Many elderly people who live on their own simply need someone to talk with
- You may be good at organising others – consider helping with the administration in a charity office or headquarters
- You might have wonderful ideas for making money – get involved in the fund-raising aspect of charities and organisations

20

What are my weaknesses?

Be realistic and honest about your abilities. Some people work better with those of their own age, others communicate well with the elderly or the really young. If you lose patience easily when dealing with children, then say so.

If you're not a 'people person' you could get involved in the research or administration side of causes, or you could work with animals. There are many different positions that can be hugely beneficial. How about working in radio stations in Africa, or a placement raising awareness for the fight against HIV and AIDS in Russia?

You shouldn't rule out travelling abroad just because you don't speak any other languages. You'll be surprised how quickly you can pick up the basics of a new language when you're living in the country.

What regions do I want to work in?

Think about the type of environment in which you'd like to work – do you prefer urban or rural areas? Do you need to be near the water at all times or would you prefer to work inland or in a mountainous or desert region?

It's very important to consider the climate in your country of choice as this will have a huge impact on you and your health. Acclimatising can take a lot of your strength. Remember that you will be spending a great deal of time in this place and if it's not the type of environment you're comfortable in, you won't enjoy it.

While most gappers automatically think of going abroad to volunteer, it isn't always necessary for you to travel outside your own country to help others. There are countless charities and causes within the UK that value volunteer workers, meaning that you wouldn't have to move too far from home if you didn't want to. If you're the type of person who needs to be close to home and loved ones, you could always volunteer in your local town with organisations such as the RSPCA or St John Ambulance.

Becoming a virtual volunteer is also an option – this involves researching and writing business proposals and press releases, all of which can be done from the comfort of your home computer.

If you do want to travel abroad for your placement but want to see more than just one place, you could raise money for a charity by getting involved in a sponsored activity. There are several charities that organise walks (or runs) along the Great Wall of China or cycle-treks through Vietnam to get much-needed funds and to increase awareness for their cause.

There are volunteer opportunities around the world in every country. Don't think that just because a country is relatively prosperous that they don't require volunteer workers. The US, for example, has great divides between rich and poor sectors and relies on volunteer agencies for many things.

Do I have any physical limitations?

Be practical about what you can and can't do. If you have a medical condition such as diabetes or epilepsy, you need to make sure that you will have access to the medication you need at all times, and that the people you will be in contact with understand any constraints you will be under and how to treat any complications that may arise. You shouldn't be discriminated against because of this but practical considerations must be taken into account.

If you have a specific dietary need – for example, if you're kosher or a coeliac – you should ensure that you will be able to get the food you require. In some cases, your meals will be provided by the community or family with whom you're living and it may not be convenient or possible for them to cook a separate meal for you. This will also depend on the country you visit – for example, if you're a vegetarian you will have several meal options in India but hardly any in Mongolia. Check out the possibilities that are available for you before you leave home.

What aspect of my job or studies do I enjoy the most?

Whatever field you're in, there will be some part of it that you love, something that makes you turn up in the morning. It could be that you enjoy the creative element, such as writing or designing, or that you like meeting people. You can use whatever aspect of your job or studies that makes you feel good in your volunteer placement. If you enjoy doing it, you'll be more enthusiastic and will get more out of it.

What skills do I have?

Even the youngest gappers have skills that can help others. Being able to speak the language of your placement country can be a big advantage. Practical qualifications are also of benefit, for example it would be useful to have a medical qualification if you want to work in healthcare. However, it's not always essential. 'Candystriping' is an American programme where teenagers volunteer in hospitals and retirement homes. Their duties involve reading to patients, bringing flowers or pictures to brighten up the rooms, handing out drinks and being there for the patients who get little attention from the medical personnel.

- Are you a creative person – do you enjoy drawing or making things? You could brighten up the lives of orphaned children in Egypt.
- Do you like cooking? You could help in homeless shelters in your own country.
- Are you observant and patient? You could count meerkats in the Kalahari desert.

What sort of projects have I been involved with in the past?

This could be anything from the cake sale you were involved with at school to the sponsored walk you did with your workmates. Every project teaches you valuable skills that you can, in turn, use during your placement. It also shows that you are aware of the world around you and that you are willing to give your time and energy to help others, which will be an advantage at the application stage.

How much time can I give?

It's up to you to decide how long you want to spend volunteering, although many organisations such as VSO will have a minimum time commitment to ensure you really make a difference. You may decide that devoting the twelve months of your gap year is the right thing for you or that you'd prefer to have some free time at the beginning to earn money to fund your trip or at the end to go travelling a bit more. You can organise your fund-raising, volunteering and travelling so that you get the most out of your year.

What roles can I fill?

These are some typical roles you could fill during your volunteer placement. Don't rule out other possibilities and don't worry if you can't see anything that suits you – if you want to join a project, you could begin in one role and gradually progress into another or suggest an alternative way that you can help.

Fund-raiser

This is one area where almost all charities need help: volunteering your time and passion to encourage others to give money. A fund-raiser needs to build strong relationships with companies and donors to raise money while applying marketing strategies for effective campaigns. As a volunteer you will be expected to work with salaried staff and other volunteers to organise fund-raising schemes and special events, give talks to promote awareness and take part in activities such as sponsored walks, themed parties and charity auctions.

Counsellor

To be a volunteer counsellor you will need to be open-minded and a good listener. It could mean spending time with people in difficult circumstances, for example prisoners. Your role will be listening to people's problems, helping them to gain perspective on their situation. You will be dealing with people either over the phone in call centres or face-to-face in a company's or charity's offices. You should have a project leader or supervisor who will advise and guide you in all situations.

Teaching assistant

A Western education is usually sufficient to teach children in poorer parts of the world, where they require classes in basic English and maths as well as practical lessons, such as how to polish your shoes and what to do if a snake is in your house. In most cases you will work alongside a qualified teacher or group of teachers, assisting them with their students, perhaps taking small groups on your own to work with. There will be some instances where you will be required to teach full classes but you should always have the support of a coordinator who will help you with any problems or queries.

Carer or companion

Not everybody needs 24-hour, hands-on care. Very often, people just need extra support – someone to talk to, who will help them with everyday tasks they find difficult. You don't need specialist qualifications but you will need to be patient, understanding, friendly and a good listener.

Publicity officer

There are so many worthwhile causes that it is very easy for one cause to slip through the net. This is where publicity officers become involved. By attracting media attention to the cause and thus raising awareness, you can promote the cause, gain public interest and generate donations.

Chapter 3

Looking for a project

With a myriad of causes to choose from it can be difficult to decide what to do. Ask yourself what kinds of projects you can join and what's involved in each. Try to refine your search further by considering where you feel you'd like to contribute. There are volunteer positions available in agencies dealing with poverty, the homeless, disaster relief and minority groups to name just a few areas. You could work alongside a family to build shelters in Chile or help to maintain historical sites in Greece and Turkey. You could work with animal conservation or the environment.

Working with communities

There are a variety of ways that you can volunteer in communities, working with children, the elderly and those with special needs as well a host of other projects. You could teach valuable skills in a school or community centre. The projects can be based in clinics or hospitals, residential or private homes. Various organisations help children who suffer from poverty, disease, injustice and violence, both on a long-term and a short-term basis.

Here are some examples of projects you could join and typical duties involved in each:

Looking after children

You could work in an orphanage where the
children are often left to simply survive with
little stimulation and no love. Romania is one
place you can choose to work with young
children in an orphanage. Your duties will be
similar in all cases:

- Getting the children dressed in the
  mornings and at bedtime
- Bathing the children and cleaning their
  sleeping areas
- Providing meals throughout the day – this
  may involve cooking as well as feeding
  the very young children
- Putting the children to bed at night and
  for naps during the day

Working with young children

You could entertain young children by playing games and organising fun activities: you might introduce games from your childhood like hopscotch or blind man's bluff; play football or make figurines with plasticine; get the children to draw pictures or make puppets. You could get the children to help you paint a mural on the walls, to brighten up their surroundings and give them something fun to do while helping them to express themselves. Try to have games that have an educational context – everybody learns faster when they're having fun. Alternatively (with permission from your project leaders) you could organise picnics and days out.

Teaching

You could teach conversational English, sports, computers, maths or basic science to children and adults with poor access to education. You don't always have to be a qualified teacher; sometimes it's enough to pass on the skills you have learned yourself. People in disadvantaged countries are often eager to learn as a way of getting a better chance in life, and they will be interested in you because you are different. This could be one of the most important ways to help a society help itself. Of course, it will be a great boost to your skills if you are considering teaching as a profession.

Working with the elderly

There are many opportunities for volunteering with the elderly at home but if you would prefer to volunteer abroad, you could help in communities in Iceland or China, for example.

As a home help for the elderly, your duties could include:

- helping with shopping – either doing the shopping for them and delivering it to the house or taking the person to the shops and helping them as they choose their groceries
- helping around the house – with cleaning, cooking and laundry
- talking to the person
- helping them to wash and dress themselves

Alternatively you could be running social events for the elderly, preparing lunches, art or gardening workshops, or even putting together a heritage project to preserve people's memories of an event in the past, encouraging community respect for its older generation. You might be helping minority groups within the community who feel excluded.

Working with those with special needs

You can choose to work with children or adults with special needs – this could be anything from learning difficulties to physical disabilities. In Morocco or India, for example, there are projects reaching out to young people with physical and mental disabilities to help them with social integration. Volunteers help with education and practical knowledge, and so those with skills in physiotherapy, occupational therapy and psychology are encouraged to apply, as well as those with an interest in sports, art, music, dance and drama. You will need to provide support and be a friend for the young people to talk to, while also helping them to be self-sufficient.

Working in healthcare

If you have a medical or nursing qualification, you can contribute directly to causes by travelling to treat those affected by illnesses, natural disasters and wars, or indirectly by training others in healthcare practices. Be aware that the areas where your skills will be most prized could be in dangerous or hostile locations.

If you don't have the necessary qualifications to work in healthcare, or don't want to work in hospitals or clinics, you could contribute by raising awareness of particular diseases, famine or drought, or by working to secure money for research, food and medical supplies.

Working with animals

If you're more of an animal lover than a people person, take advantage of the countless opportunities to work with exotic creatures around the world. Different projects have different goals, but you must have a love of the animals and enthusiasm for providing care and attention as well as an appreciation for conservation and environmental considerations.

Found in Borneo and Sumatra, the orang-utan is one of the most endangered species in Malaysia because its natural habitat is under attack and it continues to be hunted. Working at a rehabilitation centre for injured or orphaned orang-utans will mean caring for them and teaching them to survive until they are strong enough to be released back into the wild.

You could work in an elephant orphanage in Sri Lanka, caring for abused elephants, or help conservationists monitor macaws in the Peruvian Amazon. There are scientific and conservation projects around the world that accept volunteers. Most volunteers will deal with day-to-day aspects of looking after the animals, rather than specialised research or veterinary work.

You can work with all sorts of species, and for many programmes all you will need is a love of animals and nature. Whether you want to care for penguins in Africa or look after tropical birds in Costa Rica, your basic duties could include:

- feeding and watering
- monitoring behaviour – either in the wild or while the animal is in captivity

- cleaning out pens/cages/stables
- exercising the animals
- caring for injured animals
- rehabilitating animals for release back into the wild

You should be willing to get your hands dirty and you should expect some element of administrative work as records and databases will need to be maintained.

If you'd prefer a marine-based placement, volunteer for one of the projects observing turtles in Brazil, help with coral reef conservation in Fiji or join marine naturalists on a yacht studying basking sharks in the Inner Hebrides. You will need to have some diving experience in order to observe coral reefs and you should ensure that the organisation you work with will provide adequate equipment, training and support.

Working with the environment

If you care about your environment and want to use your gap year to do something practical to help, join one of the projects aimed at raising environmental awareness in Micronesia or those monitoring rainforests in Sri Lanka. Your duties will vary from project to project but you will gain valuable experience in some of the most beautiful places on the planet.

Be prepared to:

- monitor plants, trees, butterflies, insects and spiders
- construct and maintain nature trails through forests to ensure that visitors don't damage the fragile ecosystem

- mend fences, bridges and signs
- work in nurseries, looking after soil and seedlings that will be reintroduced to parts of the rainforest
- get involved in reforestation
- you may also be asked to teach English to locals and give guided tours or talks to tourists and visitors

Working in eco-tourism

Tourism is a huge industry and is one way that local people can make a living. However, introducing large numbers of people to an area can have a negative effect on the environment, damaging the ecosystem and disturbing delicate balances between flora and fauna. Sustainable development and eco-tourism are key to maintaining our environment and making sure that we don't lose our rainforests or coral reefs, endanger more plants and animals or destroy the local way of life. Countries such as Costa Rica and Mexico value volunteers who are willing to work in eco-tourism, conserving the environment and educating locals and tourists. The work involved will be similar to that of conservation work – you will monitor trees, animals, trails, signposts as well as update maps for visitors and locals. You will also be required to maintain public areas by mending fences and gates.

Searching to find out what's available

Once you've given some thought to destinations and types of volunteer work, you have to decide upon the particular organisation to apply to. Your decision will depend on many factors including, simply, availability.

The research stage can take a lot of time, which is why you should start planning your trip early. The more time you have to research your placement, the better it will work out for everyone involved.

Use the Internet

Searching for volunteer opportunities on the Internet can be time-consuming. You need to develop a system so that you don't get lost within the web of pages and links and come out the other end with a subscription for a film magazine and ten jokes about cats, but no potential placements.

- Perform specific keyword searches relevant to your interests, referring to the notes you've made from the previous chapters, rather than typing in vague terms like 'volunteer placements'. Choose the 'advanced search' option to filter out unwanted results. The results themselves could also bring up keywords that you could try in your next search.

- Bookmark useful pages that you might want to come back to at a later stage. There is nothing more frustrating than having a vague memory of something you read but later realise it could be of great use.
- Keep a list of updated information from your web searches, noting the benefits and drawbacks of each project and company, to keep track of those organisations you may want to approach.
- Join online discussion forums to post queries to other volunteers. Often you will come across topics that debate opinions on different companies.

Use newspapers

Get into the habit of reading career-related articles. Find out which supplements may focus on the voluntary sector. Most will supply contact details for relevant companies you could approach.

- On Wednesdays the society section of the *Guardian* has articles and features on social care and the environment.
- Keep up to date on current social issues, to help you to identify what sort of areas you want to become involved in.

Read books

Browse the travel section to find first-hand accounts by people who have completed volunteer placements overseas. Read books set in the places you might want to go. You will get a sense of the hardships and the rewards that you could encounter, and you may be inspired in a direction that hadn't occurred to you before when you read about someone else's experiences.

Specialist publications – subscribe to magazines like the *Voluntary Sector* magazine, which contain stories of volunteers and their past experiences, giving advice on where to go and where to avoid.

Go to volunteer 'job shops'

These centres assist with organising and advertising local volunteer opportunities. Even if you wish to volunteer elsewhere or abroad, it would be useful to visit your local centre, as you will often have the chance to speak with someone who has experience of dealing with volunteer projects on a day-to-day basis.

Attend volunteer organisation open days

This is the perfect opportunity to meet with the organisers of the programmes, who give talks on different aspects of what they offer. You will be able to talk with returned volunteers as well as those who are considering doing a placement themselves. It is a chance for you to ask about any concerns you might have and find out more about the company. Look out for dates on their websites or request to see their brochures.

Chapter 4

Applying

Your application

You should treat the application process for a
volunteer position in much the same way you
would treat that for a full-time, paying job.
If a company or project has an application
procedure in place, it's a good sign that the
company is well run and that your application
will be taken seriously.

Pay attention to the following details:

- What's involved in the application process?
- Are there forms to be filled in?
- Will there be an interview or series of interviews?
- Will you be expected to travel to their headquarters or could you participate in a telephone interview?
- How long will the process take, from sending back the form to finding out if you've been successful?

Must I sign a contract?

Always read any contracts or agreements carefully before you sign anything. If you need to, take it away and talk it over with someone you trust and make sure you understand everything.

You may also need to sign a waiver or disclaimer to indemnify the company against any injuries you may suffer during your placement – in some cases the disclaimer may be part of your application form. You should always keep copies of all documents for your own records.

The interview

The usual rules apply when it comes to interviews: you should arrive on time, looking smart with a list of questions you want answered. Make sure that you research the company thoroughly so that you're prepared for any questions they may ask you – the application form may give you clues to the types of questions you will be asked. You should also ask on forums for advice for the interview and on particular companies.

Here are some key questions:

What is the cause?

It is surprising how many people do not fully understand the nature of what they are volunteering for. Consider why it is a cause. Will you be helping to clean out a lake because it has an historical importance to the community, or is it to restore a watering hole for migrating birds?

You should also ask what the company is getting out of the project – will all the money raised for a charity go to the people it purports to help or will a large percentage be held back for 'admin fees'?

Who will I be helping?

Will you be helping the victims of a natural disaster who have lost their homes and belongings? How? By building shelters? By cooking meals? By bringing medical and food supplies into the area? Very often after a country suffers a natural disaster such as an earthquake, they need hands-on assistance in overcoming the difficulties.

On the other hand, some companies offer volunteer work that involves working on farms, for example, in the Australian outback. Be careful – in some of these cases, the only people gaining from your hard work will be the owners of the farms who need helpers but don't want to pay them.

What work has this organisation done to help?

Look back at what the company has done to contribute. Consider how their work has contributed to developments of the cause and what their intentions are for the future. Find out how their input is sustained over a period of time. This information can be found in mission statements and objectives and case studies on past projects. The company organisers should be happy to provide you with all the information you require.

How long will the placement last?

The length of placement varies from company to company and from project to project but most advise that you plan to spend at least two weeks in a community because this will give you more time to bond with the people and really make a difference. Choose the project and the length of time that suits you; you can always move on to another project once your first one is completed.

When can I go?

Some projects have particular start dates to make it easier to coordinate people, accommodation, tools and equipment. These are usually spread throughout the year. This is another reason to start planning your gap year volunteer placements as early as possible – if you leave it too late, you may miss important deadlines and lose out on your dream placement. Always have a backup placement in mind. Just because you don't get your first choice doesn't mean that your second won't be worthwhile and enjoyable.

What will I be doing on a day-to-day basis?

Before you sign on with the project find out what you will be doing each day and what your responsibilities will be. Depending on the type of project you want to join, you could be digging foundations for houses, updating trail maps or diving to observe coral reefs – even helping with administration or making the tea is a valuable contribution. Some placements may give you the chance to work at different tasks, for example in Peru you can spend time with street children, teaching them basic English and playing games, as well as building rudimentary shelters to keep them off the streets. This is one option you could consider if you'd like to contribute as much as you can to a cause while gaining experience of different types.

Will I have regular working hours?

You might not be getting paid but you do have rights.

Will your working hours change from day to day? Most companies will ensure that their volunteer workers have regular working hours and time off. You could be expected to work four hours a day or twelve – make sure that you're prepared before you get there.

You should also ask about breaks throughout the day, who will provide meals while you're working and if you will have time off during the evenings and weekends. Use your free time to explore the country and make the most of your trip by learning as much as you can about the people and the culture. Ask your hosts for advice on where to go.

What will be my level of responsibility?

Whatever project you choose, ask what the 'chain of command' is – who will be responsible for you and who you will be responsible for. Most schools will have qualified teachers who will teach you the syllabus, help you with lesson plans and give you advice on dealing with children. Building projects will have project managers to coordinate the local workers and volunteers in their groups, as well as organise delivery of materials and equipment. Conservation projects will be led by scientists and ecologists who will assign tasks appropriate to volunteers' levels of experience. Qualified doctors and nurses will supervise your work if you choose to volunteer in a healthcare project.

Will I be working alongside anyone?

What about the other participants – will they be volunteers or locals? What's the average age of the other volunteers? Is there an age limit or minimum age?

Asking these questions will give you an idea of the people you'll spend time with during your placement. Some projects have a minimum age limit because they require candidates with a little more life experience.

It is important that you have support, even though you will be expected to use your initiative while working as part of a team.

Is there an orientation meeting and training at home before the placement begins?

It's always helpful to meet the project organisers as well as your fellow volunteers. This will give you the chance to ask those last few questions, make friends and get to know the project better before you leave home. You will often be allowed to bring another person such as a parent to the meeting so that they can set their minds at ease before you depart into the unknown.

Some projects may require specific training, for example language skills or brief lessons in the history of the country and the cause. Take advantage of these courses – organisations run them for a good reason.

What support network is in place in the destination country?

Find out if you will have a mentor or guide to help you through your placement, and if they will be local (on hand for immediate assistance) or UK-based (helpful but on the other end of a phone line).

If you are travelling with an organisation, there may be someone responsible for providing practical guidance and emotional support. The support provided can vary from company to company as some may provide continued assistance throughout your placement, while others give a brief lesson on safety before you begin and then leave you alone.

How many volunteers pull out before the end of their placement?

Be wary if a lot of volunteers pull out before their placement ends. This could indicate that the company isn't telling you everything about the project. Find out before you go so that you aren't faced with any nasty surprises on your arrival.

Is it possible to contact returned volunteers by post, phone, e-mail or in person before going on the placement?

If organisations hold a meeting before the project starts, they will invite returned volunteers along to give a talk and tell the new volunteers about their experiences. They will often give you more personal knowledge of the project and will tell you the good bits as well as the bad bits that the company doesn't want to think about. They will help you to be prepared.

Does a representative from the company visit the project at any time?

You should ask how often a representative from the company visits the project, if a representative will visit during your placement and if you will have the opportunity to meet with them. It's a good sign if a representative visits the project regularly because this shows the company's continued enthusiasm for the project, their interest in the day-to-day running and in the volunteers.

Will I be able to contact home easily?

In the modern age of technology we have become accustomed to maintaining easy and immediate contact with family and friends. However, in some developing countries, the communications networks aren't as sophisticated. Monsoons can cut off communication services. The company will be able to advise you on how you can contact home and whether you'll have access to the Internet and reliable phones. Some companies may have procedures in place to contact your parents upon your safe arrival at your placement as well as means of contacting them in cases of emergency.

Talk with your phone company to ask about international calls with your current mobile – there are different contracts available that can offer free time abroad, or try pre-paid phone cards. Avoid reverse charging whenever possible as it is usually very expensive.

What happens if I'm unhappy – can I leave or go somewhere else?

All companies work very hard to place people in the project that best suits their abilities but clashes can occur. In order to ensure this doesn't happen, be honest about what you think you can do – though don't underestimate yourself. If you don't think you could work with animals or would be uncomfortable in a third-world hospital, for example, say so. No one will think the worse of you and there are lots of projects where you will fit in and make a difference. If you end up in a placement that's unbearable, you'll want to know if you can leave. This is something to ask the company up front.

Can I leave if there's a family or a national emergency?

Although most companies will try to cater for unforeseen circumstances, you ought to remember that they are relying on you for the length of your placement. They won't force you to stay against your will but they will be willing to accommodate only genuine emergencies. However sad it may be, the death of the family pet may not be sufficient to get you out of the placement.

You should heed all warnings given by the Foreign and Commonwealth Office. They will post details of countries where there is political or military unrest and may advise you to stay out of particular regions. Companies will also advise if different areas are too unsettled for projects to go ahead.

Will I get a refund if I pull out before or during the placement?

In most cases you will be asked to pay a non-refundable deposit when you send your application form. Some companies may offer a deposit refund for filling in an evaluation form upon your return – your feedback will help them to fine-tune their organisation, making sure that more volunteers have a wonderful and productive time. Once you've started your placement, you more than likely won't receive a refund if you pull out of the placement early unless there are mitigating circumstances, a serious complaint regarding the running of the project for example. Ask the company under which conditions they would consider refunding your fee.

Chapter 5

The practicalities

Figure out what you will need to organise and what the company will provide. Remember that processing paperwork always takes longer than you expect and that this is not just a holiday so there will be more details than usual to attend to before you leave.

Your finances

Setting up a budget for your placement is essential and you should already be putting money aside while you're researching projects and companies. Making just one sacrifice, such as bringing a home-made lunch instead of buying food every day will add to your gap-year nest egg.

You could also raise funds by doing a sponsored car wash, having a car boot sale (which has the added benefit of making you de-clutter your house, making it easier to store your belongings) or getting donations from local companies. Perhaps your local newspaper will sponsor you in return for a feature or a column in their social section.

Although getting a loan may sound like the easiest solution, remember that you won't be earning money while you're away and won't have any spare funds to start paying back the loan on your return.

As well as budgeting for the project fee, travel, accommodation and food, you should budget for your spending money, emergency money and any supplies you will need to take with you (these will include medical supplies as well as clothing and items such as sleeping bags and backpacks).

Why do I have to pay a project fee?

Most companies organising projects around the world require volunteers to pay to join their projects. While this contribution (often in excess of £1,000) may seem expensive, remember that often companies and charities are not government sponsored and as such receive no funding other than the goodwill of its patrons and donations from the public and volunteers. On shorter volunteering holidays working with animals, the fee may be partly a charitable donation to fund research.

You should ask for a detailed breakdown of how the money is used – i.e. how much will go to the project and how much will be held back for administration fees.

Some long-term placements may pay you expenses, though this will probably be just enough to cover your basic living costs.

What do I get for my money?

Make sure you know exactly what you're paying for and what extras you'll be responsible for. Ask what's included in your fee: travel; accommodation; food; insurance; documentation. As a rule you will be responsible for your spending money and any extra activities such as 'tourist' travel or sports and you should budget accordingly.

Your documentation

Most companies will expect you to organise your visa and residence permits. They should tell you exactly what you need to get and how to go about obtaining the necessary documentation, but all payments are your responsibility. A holiday visa won't be enough if you intend to work abroad, even if you aren't getting paid during your placement.

In the event that you need to provide proof of your plans for your stay, the company will be able to provide a special visa support letter. Be aware that they may have to send this letter directly to the embassy or consulate rather than as part of your visa application pack. You should also bear in mind that it may take a long time to organise paperwork – apply in plenty of time, putting all the necessary information on the form and making sure you fill it in accurately. If there are any problems with your application it will delay approval for your visa and may disrupt your travel plans.

As a European citizen, you are entitled to work in other EU countries without a visa, although some countries may require you to have a residence permit to stay for an extended length of time. To volunteer in most European countries, however, you will need to be fluent in the native language before they will consider giving a position to a foreigner.

You may have more difficulties securing a volunteer position in North America because the visa requirements are very strict. You will need to have an employer who is willing to sponsor you and help you with the red tape. However, summer camps operate throughout most of the US and these will employ foreign volunteers and organise working visa documentation.

Your accommodation

Any accommodation provided by projects will be, by necessity, basic. Be prepared to camp out in spare buildings, hostels or thatched huts, share with other volunteers or live with a local family. Take a good sleeping bag and tent (if necessary) as well as locks for your backpack and other bags. Just because you're there to help doesn't mean that others won't help themselves to your belongings. Check that there will be working facilities for washing (personal and laundry), cooking, heating and air conditioning.

Local families often host volunteers as a means of making extra money so don't expect them to wait on you hand and foot. However, it is an excellent way to learn the culture and the language.

What happens if I don't like the accommodation?

The nature of volunteer work means that you won't be living in the lap of luxury and you should be prepared to deal with that. If you're very unhappy with the situation, talk to your project leader to see what alternatives are available. But don't forget that you are there to help and that, while organisations will do what they can to make you happy, the project comes first.

How far will I be expected to travel from my accommodation to my workplace and what methods of travel are available?

Some projects are located in remote locations and you will be expected to either hike up hills or use public transportation to get to where you need to be. If you will need to use public transportation during your placement, find out the costs, the timetable and the transfer times. You should also ask how far your accommodation will be from the pick-up and drop-off points. Ideally your commute should allow enough time to relax at the end of the day and perhaps get involved in local activities.

Will meals be provided?

Some organisations will arrange for meals to be provided either at your accommodation or by locals who want to earn more money. The meals will be basic and native to the area. Expect to broaden your palate and try new things. If you have a special dietary requirement, find out if you will have access to cooking facilities to prepare your own meals.

Your travel

Ask what travel arrangements need to be made. In most cases, the organisation will organise the internal transfers, that is collecting you from the airport and transporting you to your accommodation, but leave the international flights to you. Remember that if international flights aren't included in the project fee, this will be an extra cost that you must include in your budget.

Ask the company to recommend a travel agent and route – they will know the closest airports and the best ones to book with. They may also have a system set up with a travel agent whereby any volunteer they recommend to the agency gets a discount.

It's important to shop around. Who knows? You might find a better deal elsewhere.

Just make sure you get the dates and the airports right.

If you don't like flying or if you intend to travel before your placement begins, it may be possible to travel to the project by other means – by ferry or overland by train or bus. Ask where the nearest ferry ports and bus and rail stations are so that you can plan your trip accordingly.

Your insurance

Paying out to provide for something that only 'may' happen may seem like a tiresome expense but it is worth it. Ask the company's advice on what cover you will need and for recommended brokers. Again, you should shop around and research the best deals. Provide the broker with all the information you have, as your policy will be invalidated if you forget any details.

The main things to be covered under your policy are travel, health and possessions but you should take out adequate insurance to cover all eventualities.

Make sure you're covered for the following:

• Travel – cancellation or delay of flight, missed flight

- Health – falling ill, suffer an accident or attack, hospital visits
- Possessions – loss or theft of possessions including documents such as your passport and bank cards

Read your policy carefully: it should cover your destination (some regions may be classed as 'tense' and may not be covered); all activities you intend to take part in (including sports); and your length of stay (holiday insurance policies generally have brief maximum stay clauses).

Don't forget that in cases of emergency you may need a family member to come out to you to bring you home and that your policy must cover this or they will have to pay their travel and accommodation expenses.

Your wardrobe

The weather will determine many of the items you will need and you should ask the company's advice on the appropriate clothes to bring. However hot the country may be, shorts, T-shirts and flip-flops aren't always suitable. For example, in jungles and rainforests, it's advisable to wear sturdy boots and full-length trousers because it's not a good idea to expose your legs to spiders and potentially hazardous plants. Bring ample sunscreen, mosquito repellent, sunglasses and a decent first-aid kit with antiseptic cream, plasters and bandages. If you need glasses for distance or reading, you should pack a spare pair.

Your home

If you're a homeowner, you probably don't want to sell your house just because you're going away for an extended length of time. One way to make sure your property remains safe and that the mortgage is paid is to let the house. It's usually best to place your property in the hands of a professional property management company – they will vet all tenants, take care of any problems and ensure that the rent is paid promptly and in full.

If you choose, you could ask a friend or a family member to take care of the property for you, but be careful. It's a lot of responsibility and it may cause strained relations upon your return.

Your furniture

You can let the property fully-furnished but if you do have any expensive items or anything of sentimental value, you should make sure that they're safe from harm or accidental damage. Store personal belongings in a safe place, such as a loft with a secure lock, or in the garage or loft of a friend or family member.

In some cases you will still need to store furniture. You can lend a friend the furniture for the length of your placement; store it in a family member's house; or store it in custom-built facilities. These facilities can be expensive but at least you won't spend the first week of your return squabbling with loved ones about the scratch on your favourite table.

Your car

There are several options open to you for dealing with your car. You can:

- sell it – this option may prove more expensive than it's worth, especially if you're only travelling for a few months
- declare it off road or SORN (Statutory Off Road Notification) – make sure you have somewhere secure to park it that won't be in anybody's way and that somebody you trust has a key in case of emergencies
- lend it to a friend or family member – ensure that the vehicle is taxed, has an up-to-date MOT and that the new driver is adequately insured in case of any accident. You will need to inform

your insurance company as failure
to do so may invalidate any claims. It
would also be a good idea to have a
written agreement (even between
family and friends) stating that they are
responsible for the car during your
absence, including paying for any repairs.

Your pets

Under PETS, the Pet Travel Scheme, you may be able to bring your pet to certain rabies-free countries without having to place them in quarantine on your return. The majority of these countries are holiday rather than volunteer-activity destinations, however.

Most projects won't allow you to bring pets with you on your placement because of the potential problems they can cause and the fact that you won't be able to give your full attention to the project. This is also to ensure that no other volunteers or local workers are inconvenienced. Check with individual companies for their pet policies but you'll probably want to make arrangements for your pet to stay with a friend or family member.

Chapter 6

Further preparations

While you're sorting out the practicalities of becoming a volunteer, you need to prepare yourself mentally for what's ahead of you.

Research the country

You should learn all you can about the country you have chosen to visit. This involves everything from researching the culture and customs to finding out which plants, insects and creatures are harmless and which should be left alone. Read about the country's history and the nature of the society – it will help you to understand the people and integrate more easily. Remember that people won't necessarily do things the way you're used to at home and that it can be easy to offend someone, even unintentionally.
This could be:

- Greeting people – some cultures believe in hierarchy; for example, in India you should greet the most senior person first

- The way you dress – in some countries females are expected to cover their hair or arms; in Zaire it would be acceptable for a woman to walk around topless but not to wear short shorts and show any part of her bottom
- Making physical contact – in Shanghai, people in social situations greet each other with slaps to the back, reserving the handshake for business, while a Muslim woman will never offer you her hand and you should never offer her yours. In Rio de Janeiro, maintaining eye contact is an important facet of getting to know people and showing friendliness
- Privacy requirements – different cultures have different views on privacy and in many countries whole families live together in close quarters, often sleeping in the same room

- Attitudes to smoking and alcohol – some projects may have strict no smoking and no alcohol policies that you must respect

If you make an effort and show a willingness to learn their customs, most people will forgive inadvertent mistakes.

Stay fit and healthy

Acclimatising to different temperatures, humidities and altitudes, not to mention foods and water, will make the beginning of your placement difficult. Get healthy before you go – the healthier you are, the easier you will find it to adapt and to withstand any illnesses. It's also important to be relatively fit – some countries may have rugged terrain and the projects could involve lots of walking and physical work.

Visit your doctor a few months before you go and ask about the necessary vaccinations. Some vaccinations, malaria for example, need to be taken several weeks before departure so don't leave it to the last minute. Take vitamins and mineral supplements with you and bear in mind that your system may take a while to adjust.

Topping up your skills

If you feel that you need formal training to back up your natural abilities, consider taking a course before going on your placement. The skills learned in courses such as secretarial and teaching will help you secure a volunteer position as well as a full-time job on your return. Don't forget to include any costs for courses in your budget.

- Learn the language: you will feel more confident on your first day if you can at least say 'hello', 'thank you' and 'where's the toilet?' Learning the language will also prove your interest in the country, your willingness to immerse yourself in the culture and your enthusiasm for the project and the people.

If you're going to be working on a building project, then even learning the basics, such as hammer, nail and wood, would be a good start.

Language skills, such as translating, are always in high demand in volunteer, private and public sectors.

- Administration skills are very useful in all areas of volunteer and professional life. No matter what career you choose, there will be an administrative element involved and you will need to know how to touch-type, organise filing systems, answer phones in a professional manner and work with the usual computing software systems as well as being comfortable using the Internet and e-mail.

- While a lot of volunteer teaching positions don't require candidates to have a teaching qualification or experience, a

TEFL course can help you. Besides giving you the basic know-how in communicating a topic to others who speak a different language, you can use these skills in your professional life and while you're travelling.

- Direct experience may be an advantage – if you would like to spend your gap year working with lion cubs in Zimbabwe, volunteer at an animal shelter in your local town in the months coming up to your departure. You will learn many skills you will need when dealing with animals and will have confidence before you leave home.

- Even if you don't want to volunteer in the healthcare sector, a first-aid course is always a good thing to put on your CV. It may favourably influence a company's decision when they come to

oosing candidates because they value
lunteers who are capable of responding
to minor emergencies. If you have already
decided on your placement country
before you take the course, ask your
instructor for advice in how to deal with
injuries specific to that country, for
example, spider or snake bites, or tending
to cuts and bruises with basic medical
supplies.

- Self-defence teaches you skills that you
  will hopefully never need to employ
  but it's always better to be safe than
  sorry. Don't allow yourself to be pulled
  into dangerous situations just because
  you have some knowledge of how to get
  out of them.

Checklist

You will need to budget for the following items:

- Project fee
- Visas and residence permits
- Accommodation
- Travel
- Food
- Medical supplies
- Insurance
- Spending money
- Emergency money
- Training courses

Don't forget these items:

- Passport
- Another form of photographic identification, e.g. a driver's license. If you are eligible for an International Driving Permit (IDP), apply three months before you leave
- Insurance policy documents
- Flight tickets
- Important phone numbers and e-mail addresses, i.e. bank in case of loss or theft of bank cards, and insurance company in case of emergency

Make copies of all these documents, scan them and e-mail them to yourself, so that you can access them if necessary.

Bring these items with you (in a backpack that you can carry without too much difficulty):

- Clothing, including appropriate footwear and a hat
- Phrase book and guide book
- Travel journal – to begin writing that travel memoir
- First-aid kit
- Sleeping bag
- Tent with all the necessary accoutrements: ground sheet, pegs etc (if necessary)
- Torch and batteries
- Water-purifying tablets
- Games, toys and sweets (especially if working with children)

Resources

While we cannot endorse any companies or organisations, here are a few suggestions of places to start your research:

www.vso.org.uk

www.charitychallenge.com

www.csv.org.uk

www.earthwatch.org

www.gap.org.uk

www.globalvolunteers.org

www.gvi.co.uk

www.responsibletravel.com

www.travellersworldwide.com

www.worktravelcompany.co.uk

www.yearoutgroup.org

OTHER TITLES FROM SUMMERSDALE

GAP YEAR
ADVENTURES

A Guide to Making it
a Year to Remember

Gap Year Adventures
A Guide to Making it a Year to Remember

£3.99 Pb

Your gap year stretches ahead of you, begging to be filled with sun-drenched beaches, treks through exotic landscapes and thrilling exploits. How can you plan the adventures to make the most of your time out?

This essential guide is crammed with exciting ideas from around the world, from abseiling to zorbing, diving with sharks to learning yoga from the masters. Discover how to make your gap year truly unforgettable.

BACKPACKING
SAFETY TIPS

A Guide to Enjoying
Any Trip Safely

Backpacking Safety Tips
A Guide to Enjoying Any Trip Safely

£3.99 Pb

Backpacking adventures are all too often cut short by a stolen wallet or 'Delhi belly'. Instead, you can be aware and be prepared.

These essential tips will put your mind at rest, leaving you to concentrate on making your travels the stuff of dreams.

BUTTERTEA AT SUNRISE

A Year in the Bhutan Himalaya

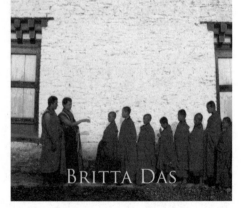

BRITTA DAS

Buttertea at Sunrise

A Year in the Bhutan Himalaya

Britta Das

£7.99 Pb

Often seen as a magical paradise at the end of the world, Bhutan is inaccessible to most travellers. Set against the dramatic scenery of the Himalaya, this beautiful memoir reveals hardships and happiness in a land almost untouched by the West.

When Britta, a young physiotherapist, goes to work as a volunteer in a remote village hospital, her good intentions are put to the test amid monsoons, fleas and shocking conditions. But as she visits homes in the mountains and learns the mysteries of tantric Buddhism, the country casts its enduring spell.

Gaining insights into the traditions of this mystical kingdom, she makes friends and falls in love. Bhutan will change her life forever.

www.summersdale.com